The MOST FAMOUS CLASSICAL MUSIC
FOR EASIER PIANO

ISBN 978-1-5400-8404-0

HAL•LEONARD®

Visit Hal Leonard Online at
www.halleonard.com

Contact us:
Hal Leonard
7777 West Bluemound Road
Milwaukee, WI 53213
Email: info@halleonard.com

In Europe, contact:
Hal Leonard Europe Limited
42 Wigmore Street
Marylebone, London, W1U 2RN
Email: info@halleonardeurope.com

In Australia, contact:
Hal Leonard Australia Pty. Ltd.
4 Lentara Court
Cheltenham, Victoria, 3192 Australia
Email: info@halleonard.com.au

Contents

(continued)

Sheep May Safely Graze
from Cantata, BWV 208

Johann Sebastian Bach
1685–1750

6

2nd time, rit. _ _ _ _ **Fine**

7

Air on the G String

from Orchestral Suite No. 3 in D Major, BWV 1068

Johann Sebastian Bach
1685–1750

Arioso
(Sinfonia)
from Canata, BWV 156

Johann Sebastian Bach
1685–1750

Badinerie

from Orchestral Suite No. 2 in B minor, BWV 1067

Johann Sebastian Bach
1685–1750

Jesu, joy of man's desiring
from Cantata, BWV 147

Johann Sebastian Bach
1685–1750

Sleepers, Awake

from Canata, BWV 140

Johann Sebastian Bach
1685–1750

Theme

from Piano Concerto No. 3 in C minor, Op. 37

Ludwig van Beethoven
1770–1827

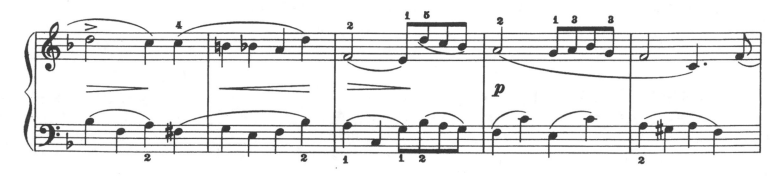

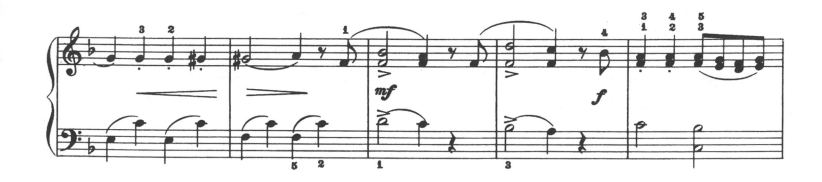

Theme

from Symphony No. 5 in C minor, Op. 67

Ludwig van Beethoven
1770–1827

Andante con moto

Theme

from Symphony No. 6 in F Major, Op. 68

Ludwig van Beethoven
1770–1827

Theme
from Symphony No. 7 in A Major, Op. 92

Ludwig van Beethoven
1770–1827

Allegretto

Ode to Joy

from Symphony No. 9 in D minor, Op. 125

Ludwig van Beethoven
1770–1827

Allegro

Themes

from *Carmen*

Georges Bizet
1838–1875

Farandole

from *L'Arlésienne* Suite No. 2

Georges Bizet
1838–1875

Minuet
from String Quintet in E Major, Op. 11, No. 5

Luigi Boccherini
1743–1805

36

D.C. Minuet
al Fine

Polovetsian Dances

from *Prince Igor*

Alexander Borodin
1833–1887

Moderato con moto

38

Nocturne
from String Quartet No. 2 in D Major

Alexander Borodin
1833–1887

Hungarian Dance in F-sharp minor

WoO 1, No. 5

Johannes Brahms
1833–1897

43

Theme

from Symphony No. 1 in C minor, Op. 68

Johannes Brahms
1833–1897

Theme

from *Variations on a Theme by Haydn*, Op. 56

Johannes Brahms
1833–1897

Lullaby
Op. 49, No. 4

Johannes Brahms
1833–1897

Tenderly

Trumpet Voluntary
(The Prince of Denmark's March)

Jeremiah Clarke
c. 1674–1707

Andante maestoso

Themes

from Symphony No. 9 in E minor, Op. 95 "From the New World"

Antonín Dvořák
1841–1904

Largo

Allegro

Allegro risoluto

Nimrod

Variations on an Original Theme, Op. 36, "Enigma Variations"

Edward Elgar
1857–1934

Pomp and Circumstance

March No. 1 in D Major, Op. 39

Edward Elgar
1857–1934

The Last Rose of Summer

from *Martha*

Friedrich von Flotow
1812–1883

Larghetto

Pavane in F-sharp minor
Op. 50

Gabriel Fauré
1845–1924

Pie Jesu

from *Requiem in D minor*, Op. 48

Gabriel Fauré
1845–1924

65

Sicilienne
Op. 78

Gabriel Fauré
1845–1924

Entrance of the Gladiators
Op. 68

Julius Fučik
1872–1916

Moderato

Ave Maria

adapted from Prelude in C Major, BWV 846 by Johann Sebastian Bach

Charles Gounod
1818–1893

Moderato

Morning
from *Peer Gynt* Suite No. 1, Op. 46, No. 1

Edvard Grieg
1843–1907

75

Anitra's Dance

from *Peer Gynt* Suite No. 1, Op. 46, No. 3

Edvard Grieg
1843–1907

Tempo di mazurka

D. C.

Solveig's Song

from *Peer Gynt* Suite No. 2, Op. 55, No. 4

Edvard Grieg
1843–1907

Theme
from Piano Concerto in A minor, Op. 16

Edvard Grieg
1843–1907

Bourée

from *Music for the Royal Fireworks*, HWV 351

George Frideric Handel
1685–1759

The Harmonious Blacksmith

(Air and Variations)
from Suite No. 5 in E Major, HVW 430

George Frideric Handel
1685–1759

Largo
(Ombra mai fu)
from *Serse*, HVW 40

George Frideric Handel
1685–1759

Where'er You Walk

from *Semele*, HVW 58

George Frideric Handel
1685–1759

This page has intentionally been left blank to facilitate page turns.

Air

from *Water Music:* Suite in F Major, HWV 348

George Frideric Handel
1685–1759

Con moto

Bourée

from *Water Music:* Suite in F Major, HWV 348

George Frideric Handel
1685–1759

Hornpipe

from *Water Music:* Suite in D Major, HWV 349

George Frideric Handel
1685–1759

Jupiter Chorale

from *The Planets*

Gustav Holst
1874–1934

Evening Prayer

from *Hansel and Gretel*

Engelbert Humperdinck
1854–1921

Adagietto
from Symphony No. 5

Gustav Mahler
1860–1911

Meditation

from *Thaïs*

Jules Massenet
1842–1912

101

Nocturne

from *A Midsummer Night's Dream*, Op. 61

Felix Mendelssohn
1809–1847

Theme
from Clarinet Concerto, K. 622

Wolfgang Amadeus Mozart
1756–1791

Minuet

from *Don Giovanni*, K. 527

Wolfgang Amadeus Mozart
1756–1791

Allegro

from *Eine kleine Nachtmusik*, K. 525

Wolfgang Amadeus Mozart
1756–1791

Rondo

from *Eine kleine Nachtmusik*, K. 525

Wolfgang Amadeus Mozart
1756–1791

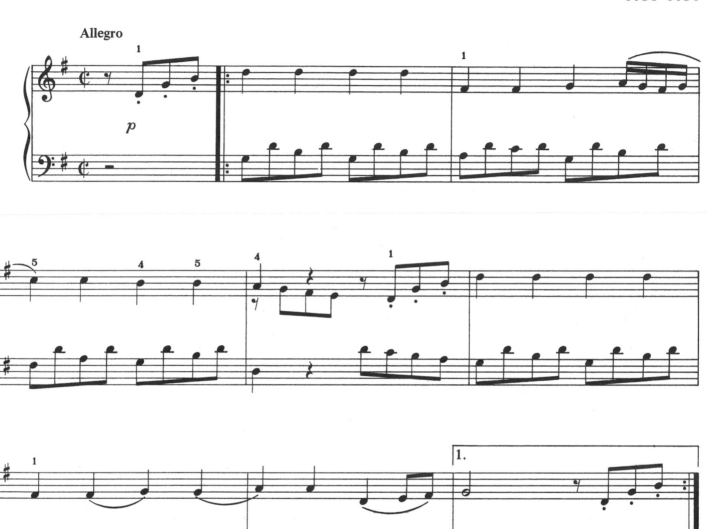

Romance

from *Eine kleine Nachtmusik*, K. 525

Wolfgang Amadeus Mozart
1756–1791

Alleluia

from *Exsultate, jubilate*, K. 165

Wolfgang Amadeus Mozart
1756–1791

Allegro non troppo

115

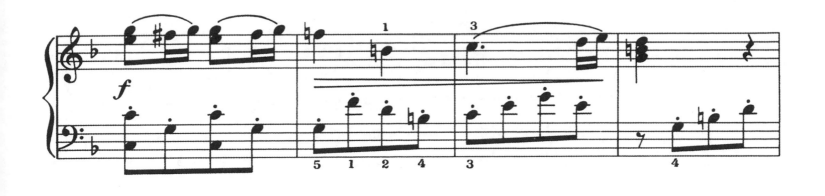

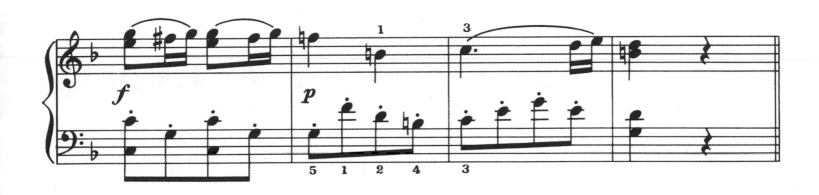

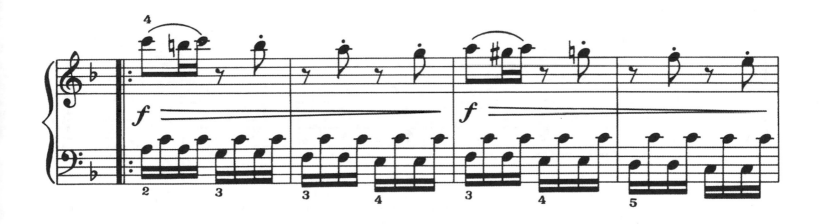

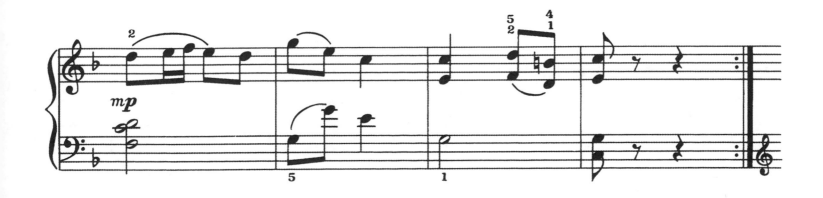

Theme
from Piano Concerto No. 20 in D minor, K. 466

Wolfgang Amadeus Mozart
1756–1791

Theme
from Piano Concerto No 21 in C Major, K. 467

Wolfgang Amadeus Mozart
1756–1791

Coda

Theme

from Symphony No. 40 in G minor, K. 550

Wolfgang Amadeus Mozart
1756–1791

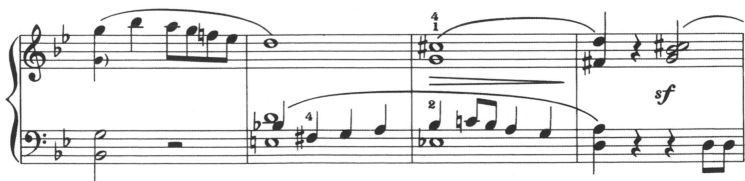

Promenade

from *Pictures at an Exhibition*

Modeste Mussorgsky
1839–1881

Caprice No. 24

from *24 Caprices*

Nicolò Paganini
1782–1840

Brightly

Can–Can

from *Orpheus in the Underworld*

Jacques Offenbach
1819–1880

Barcarolle

from *The Tales of Hoffmann*

Jacques Offenbach
1819–1880

D.S. al Fine

Canon in D

Johann Pachelbel
1653–1706

Con 8va ad lib. . . . .

138

Jerusalem

Hubert Parry
1848–1918

Over the Waves

Juventino Rosas
1868–1894

144

D. S. al fine

Dance of the Hours

from *La Gioconda*

Amilcare Ponchielli
1834–1886

DANCE OF THE HOURS OF DAY

146

ENTRANCE OF THE HOURS OF NIGHT
Moderato

p espressivo

DANCE OF ALL THE HOURS
Con molto brio

O mio babbino caro

from *Gianni Schicchi*

Giacomo Puccini
1858–1924

Themes
from *Madama Butterfly*

Giacomo Puccini
1858–1924

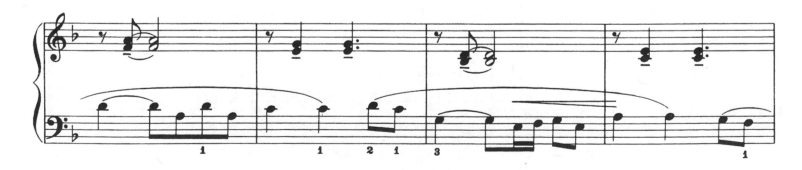

Rondeau

from *Abdelazar*

Henry Purcell
1659–1695

Themes

from *The Barber of Seville*

Gioacchino Rossini
1792–1868

Theme

from *William Tell*

Gioacchino Rossini
1792–1868

The Swan

from *The Carnival of the Animals*

Camille Saint-Saëns
1835–1921

162

Ave Maria
D. 839

Franz Schubert
1797–1828

Serenade

from *Swan Song*, D. 957, No. 4

Franz Schubert
1797–1828

Theme

from Symphony No. 8 in B minor, D. 759 "Unfinished"

Franz Schubert
1797–1828

Allegro moderato

Theme
from Symphony No. 9 in C Major, D. 944

Franz Schubert
1797–1828

To Music

D. 547

Franz Schubert
1797–1828

The Trout
D. 550

Franz Schubert
1797–1828

The Moldau

from *My Homeland*

Bedřich Smetana
1824–1884

The Liberty Bell

John Philip Sousa
1854–1932

181

The Stars and Stripes Forever

John Philip Sousa
1834–1932

Moderato

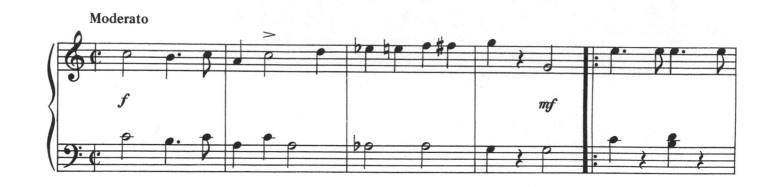

D.C. al FINE
(without repeat)

The Washington Post

John Philip Sousa
1834–1932

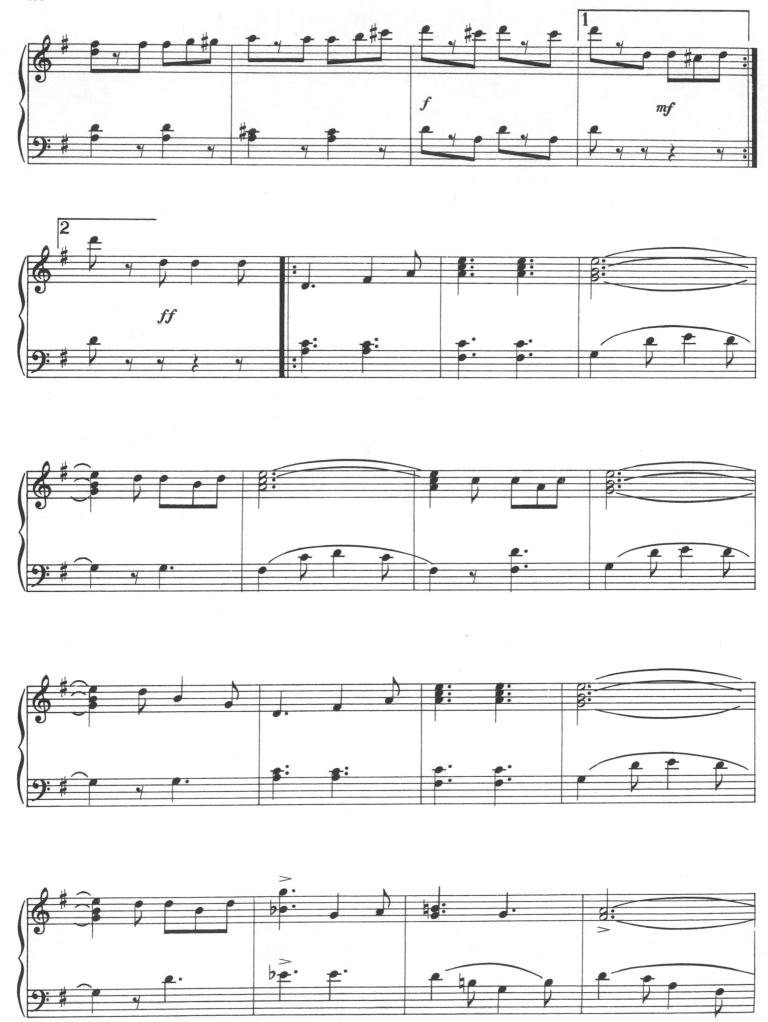

Radetzky March
Op. 228

Johann Strauss I
1804–1849

Fine

D.S. 𝄋 al Fine

Emperor Waltz
Op. 437

Johann Strauss II
1825–1899

192

On the Beautiful Blue Danube

Op. 314

Johann Strauss II
1825–1899

D.S. 𝄊
al Fine

Tales from the Vienna Woods
Op. 325

Johann Strauss II
1835–1899

Viennese Blood
Op. 354

Johann Strauss II
1825–1899

Wine, Women, and Song
Op. 333

Johann Strauss II
1825–1899

Tritsch-Tratsch Polka
Op. 214

Johann Strauss II
1825–1899

Tempo di polka

Themes

from *1812 Overture*, Op. 49

Pyotr Il´yich Tchaikovsky
1840–1893

Allegro vivace

Marche slave
Op. 31

Pyotr Il´yich Tchaikovsky
1840–1893

Dance of the Reed Flutes

from *The Nutcracker*, Op. 71

Pyotr Il´yich Thaikovsky
1840–1893

March

from *The Nutcracker*, Op. 71

Pyotr Il´yich Tchaikovsky
1840–1893

Waltz of the Flowers

from *The Nutcracker*, Op. 71

Pyotr Il'yich Tchaikovsky
1840–1893

Moderato

221

Theme
from Piano Concerto No. 1 in B-flat minor, Op. 23

Pyotr Il´yich Tchaikovsky
1840–1893

Andante non troppo e molto maestoso

Theme

from *Romeo and Juliet*

Pyotr Il´yich Tchaikovsky
1840–1893

Moderato

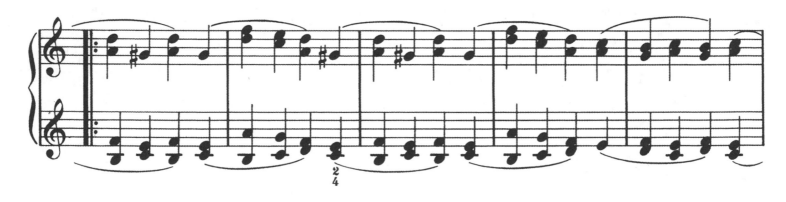

Theme

from *Swan Lake*, Op. 20

Pyotr Il´yich Tchaikovsky
1840–1893

229

Theme

from Symphony No. 5, in B minor, Op. 58

Pyotr Il´yich Tchaikovsky
1840–1893

Waltz
from *Swan Lake*, Op. 20

Pyotr Il´yich Thaikovsky
1840–1893

Tempo di valse

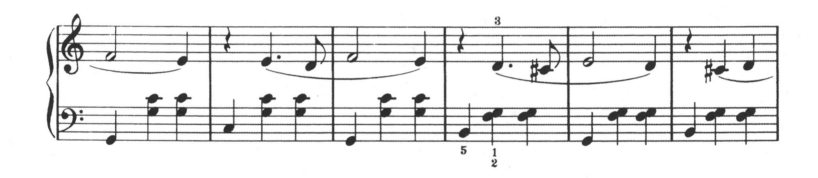

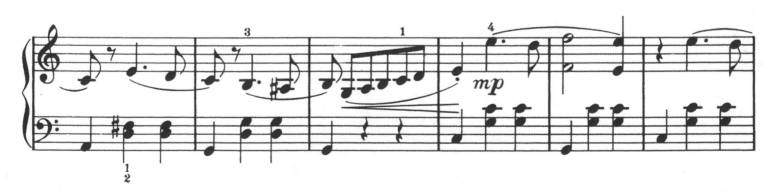

Theme
from Symphony No. 6 in E minor, Op. 64, "Pathétique"

Pyotr Il´yich Tchaikovsky
1840–1893

Grand March
from *Aida*

Giuseppe Verdi
1813–1901

237

La donna é mobile

from *Rigoletto*

Giuseppe Verdi
1813–1901

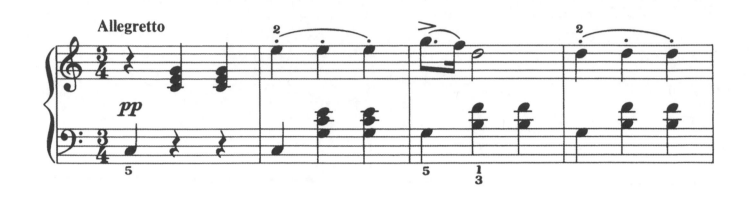

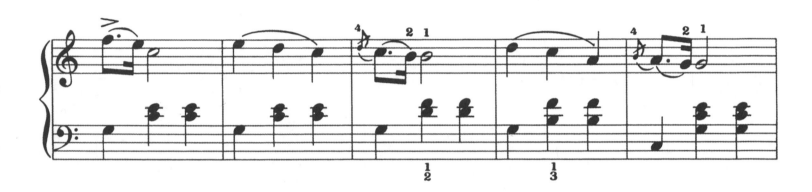

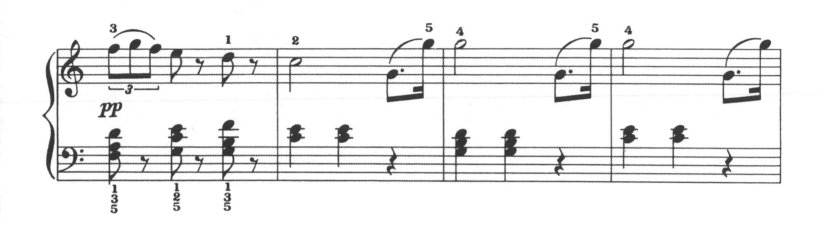

Libiamo né lieti calici

from *La Traviata*

Giuseppi Verdi
1813–1901

Skaters' Waltz

Op. 183

Emile Waldteufel
1837–1915

243

D.S. al fine

Pilgrims' Chorus
from *Tannhäuser*

Richard Wagner
1813–1883

Bridal Chorus
from *Lohengrin*

Richard Wagner
1813–1883

Moderato con moto